SELF-PUBLISHING:
MANUSCRIPT TO BESTSELLER

(Revised Edition)

PETER TREMBLAY

Agora Books
Ottawa, Canada

Self-publishing: Manuscript to Bestseller (Revised Edition)

© 2022 by Peter Tremblay

All Rights Reserved. No part of this book may be reproduced, stored in a retrieval system, or transmitted in any form or by any means, electronic or mechanical, including photocopying, recording, or otherwise without the expressed written consent of The Agora Cosmopolitan.

Care has been taken to trace ownership / source of any academic or other reference materials contained in this text. The publisher will gratefully accept any information that will enable it to rectify any reference or credit in subsequent edition(s), of any incorrect or omitted reference or credit.

Agora Books

P.O. Box 24191

300 Eagleson Road

Kanata, Ontario K2M 2C3

Agora Books is a self-publishing agency for authors that was launched by The Agora Cosmopolitan which is a registered not-for-profit corporation.

ISBN 978-1-77838-022-8

Printed in Canada

CONTENTS

Preface 1

Introduction 3
    The right mindset 4
    Make it bite-sized 5
    Organizing 6

Chapter 1: Choose Your Publishing Pathway 9
    Forms of publishing: self vs hybrid vs traditional 9
    Traditional Publishing 10
    Self-publishing 10
    Hybrid publishing 11
    How to choose 12

Chapter 2: Your Author Business Plan 13
    Mission statement 14
    Author brand and culture 14
    Ideal reader 14
    Career goals and objectives 15
    Market analysis 15
    Differentiator 16
    Financials 16
    Action steps 17

Chapter 3: Your Book's Conception 19
Getting into the right headspace 19
Finding your great inspiration 20
Make a plan and a schedule 21

Chapter 4: Your Road to Financial Success 23
Pre-marketing build-up 23
Building a premarketing plan and your target audience 24
   Set your objective 24
   Create your website 24
   Build an email list 25
   Send out newsletters 25
   Let your guard down 25
   Keep at it! 26

Chapter 5: Writing It: Executing Your Book 27
Write a book within 24 hours or more? 27
Preventing writer's block 28

Chapter 6: Ready-Set-Go: Overview of Getting Your Book Produced 31
Assistance for your self-publishing goals 32

Chapter 7: Nitty Gritty Facets of Pre-Marketing 35
Book cover design 35
Author blogs/book websites 36
Search engine optimization for authors 37
Pre-ordering strategies 38

Chapter 8: Important Production Considerations 39
ISBN registration 39
Basic copy editing 40

Advanced copy editing considerations 41
   Line editing 41
   Developmental editing 41
   Substantive Editing 42
Professional Typesetting 42
What is an eBook? 43
   eBook formatting 43
eBook formatting versus typesetting for printed copies 44
What about audiobooks? 45

Chapter 9: Formats of Books 47

Pros of paperbacks (or hardcovers) 48
Cons of paperbacks (or hardcovers) 48
Pros of eBooks 48
Cons of eBooks 49
Pros of audiobooks 49
Cons of audiobooks 49

Chapter 10: Print-On Demand Versus Printing
for An Inventory 51

Print-on-demand overview 52
Getting your self-published book available for sale 53
   IngramSpark 53
   Amazon Kindle Direct Publishing (KDP) 53
   BookBaby 54
   Blurb 54

Addendum 55
Endnotes 57

PREFACE

Are you a writer who seeks to transform your manuscript into a potential bestseller?

In the "old days," authors were largely confined to send off their manuscripts for review by corporate trade publishers with restrictive editorial policies that conspired to shut out a lot of potentially successful authors. But now, a "self-publishing revolution" is empowering new generations of authors to avail themselves of various resources to publish on their own. However, the overwhelming majority of these books are either of editorially poor quality or lack a thoughtful pre-marketing plan for success. In a notable CNET.com article titled "Self-publishing a book: 25 things you need to know," David Carnoy estimates that only about 5 percent of self-published books out there are decent, and only 1 percent are very good.

This book aims to guide self-publishing authors toward becoming among the 1 percent. You can optimize the prospects of your book by integrating the road map for success that this book outlines.

INTRODUCTION

Self-publishing a book can be a daunting task, especially when you're new to it and have to learn the ropes. Among the various elements vital to the success of a self-published book, one of the most important is self-discipline and the willingness to try out different approaches.

Today, there are a growing number of self-published authors, which is to be expected considering the numerous benefits writers enjoy when they self-publish their work. Traditional publishing methods are slowly being phased out in support of a more flexible publishing path where writers are given greater control over their message, marketing, and even pricing.

If you are a writer considering self-publishing your book, you should know that without proper guidance, achieving success as a self-published author can be difficult.

A positive endorsement of self-publishing comes from Thomishia Booker,[1] CEO of Hey Carter! Incorporated and self-published author of the *Hey Carter! Children's Book Series*. According to Booker, "there are a lot of options when it comes to self-publishing and it can become overwhelming comparing those differences without any guidance. Self-publishing platforms have made publishing easier in terms of printing the final product, but it is the work leading up to this point that can be challenging to navigate."

The self-publishing industry is rapidly evolving from what it was a few years ago. Now, there are lots of competitors who are constantly pushing out new information and publishers who are continually making necessary upgrades to their facilities, infrastructure, and pricing.

The right mindset

What if I told you that you can write and successfully self-publish a book in 24 hours? Before you think it is impossible, there are unique approaches that differ from the traditional way that most people have been taught when it comes to writing and publishing a book.

Many aspiring authors choose the more conventional method of writing and publishing their books, but due to the very low barrier of entry into the self-publishing market, anyone can now become an author. The ease of access has a downside: many self-publishers release substandard, poorly-written books into the market because they lack a certain level of quality control. This pitfall should be at the back of your mind even as you begin the first step of the publishing process—writing the book itself.

While there is no one-size-fits-all approach to writing a book, as even the traditional method can sometimes be equally effective, there is a different and proven option that is a much faster and effective way.

The best part is that not many people are aware of this approach, which definitely gives you an advantage.

The journey to writing a book is an amazing creative process, but while many people want to be writers, most fail to do so. The most common explanations for a lack of output are "I am not a very good writer," "I'm not sure anyone wants to read what I have to say," and of course, "writing a book takes too much time." While these excuses can rear their heads at any time, it's imperative that you not let these thoughts hold you back from writing the book you want to write.

One major deterrent for aspiring authors is procrastination. Every writer wants to write a book that's valuable to the reader and that leaves a long-lasting impression. This can seem like an impossible task, and that leads some aspiring authors to believe that writing a book requires too much time and too many resources. Therefore, they keep procrastinating, and eventually end up not writing, let alone publishing, their work.

Many people who want to write and publish a book get easily overwhelmed and intimated at the idea that their book has to be perfect—from grammar to spelling, book cover design and theme—and this struggle for perfection is one of the many reasons their book never sees the light of day.

Make it bite-sized

To overcome this fear, it is important to look at writing and the publishing industry in a different light from the traditional way you are familiar with. The advent of the internet has changed a lot of things, and the publishing industry hasn't been left out. Today, many people are reading and buying fewer books than during the pre-internet era. According to a 2019 Pew Research Center Report, about a quarter of Americans did not read a book in the previous year.[2]

This can be attributed to the fact that a lot of internet users have a short attention span—approximately eight seconds—and are looking to consume more bite-sized information. Platforms such as blogs, social media posts, podcasts, and even short videos are preferred as they don't require as much commitment, while the reader still benefits and gets value from consuming such content. Many people want to access information in different ways, and this transcends the traditional way of spreading information.

Social media sites like Facebook, Twitter, Instagram and even Tik-Tok have opened a whole new market where people can create and consume bite-sized content. With the declining attention span of the average human, very few people are willing to commit hours, days, and even months of their lives reading a 400-page book. Within this playing field, there are still readers out there, eager for what you have to share with them. But the takeaway is to understand that you need to follow a much different approach than you may otherwise have though; the new market allows you to create a book that is a lot shorter and easier to create, while still delivering the expected value, but in a more succinct way.

A book doesn't have to contain over 300-pages to provide value to the reader. In fact, there are a lot of books in the market today that are very wordy, but with as much as 90 percent of the content being utter nonsense—and no reader wants to endure that.

Often, writers want to be more expressive by including different stories and scenarios that reinforce their point and immerse the reader into their experiences—whether fictional or not. But even in the movie industry, a lot of production companies have realized that not many viewers enjoy watching 2-to-3 hours long movies, and companies like Netflix now provide "bite-sized entertainment" in the form of TV series. Publishing platforms have followed suit, marketing "short reads" categories that contain short stories and non-fiction that readers can consume in a single sitting.

So, it is important to understand that a book doesn't have to be lengthy for it to be good or valuable. You could create a book with under 50 pages and have it become more impactful than one that is over 500-pages long.

Organizing

The key to achieving this kind of success is to be certain of the specific message you intend to pass across with your book, focusing on the most important parts and outlining into different chapters. When you break down a book into more structured bits, where you define the overall theme of each chapter and the top three things you want it to be centred around, finishing it in a shorter window of time becomes a lot more achievable. Once you've immersed yourself into the ideas you're working with as a writer or content creator, it becomes a lot easier to go with the flow and complete the book in 24 hours or less.

One common writing principle that will help you to avoid writer's block is to not seek perfection. Many writers suffer from perfectionism, which is quite damaging especially during a first draft.

Experienced editor Lauren Hughes warns that "blocks often occur because writers put a lot of pressure on themselves to sound 'right' the first time. A good way to loosen up and have fun again in a draft is to give yourself permission to write imperfectly."[3]

Always remember that you can always go back and make whatever necessary edits once you're done writing. For the draft phase, just focus on pouring the ideas in your head into words, no matter how disorganized they may appear. Remember: nothing is ever truly perfect, so don't waste time and energy working toward an impossible standard for yourself.

Renowned author Dan Kennedy discusses the 80 percent approach[4] that states, 80 per cent is more than enough perfection because most of the things we worry about go unnoticed by readers. For example, while you may have published a book with a few grammatical errors, there's a high chance that as long as you have been able to successfully pass across your message, you would get rave reviews.

Writing a book doesn't have to feel like a huge chore, especially since the goal is to provide value to the readers. It is important to acknowledge the times that we are in and the different markets that exist and use this as a guide when writing and publishing a book.

CHAPTER 1

CHOOSE YOUR PUBLISHING PATHWAY

Forms of publishing: self vs hybrid vs traditional

For many aspiring authors, the path to publishing their work can be quite confusing, especially with the endless options available these days. However, if you spend quality time researching, you're bound to narrow your options down to three: self-publishing, traditional publishing, and hybrid publishing.

While these methods are the most popular, you are still left to determine which one is the best for you. Deciding your next steps is crucial to the overall success of your book, and with so many options now available, it can be very overwhelming. It's no longer enough to just focus on writing a best-selling book; choosing the right publishing platform is equally as important.

In comparison to decades ago, aspiring authors no longer have to be fully dependent on traditional publishers to strike a good book deal. But the availability of options[5] does not eliminate the need to be strategic in your publishing choice. First, you need to understand the different publishing paths.

Traditional Publishing

Traditional publishing is the oldest of the three publishing paths and most authors are quite familiar with it. Here, all the risks associated with publishing your work are managed by the publisher, and they cover the entire financial burden of launching your book into the market. A traditional publisher would pay the author an advance fee and additional royalties, which is a percentage of book sales, in exchange for exclusive rights to publish their book.

Traditional publishers pay for everything—proofreading, editing, typesetting, printing, binding, cover art design, marketing, advertising, warehousing, shipping and billing. If any publisher attempts to collect money from you, then they are not a traditional publisher.

Most traditional publishers operate from large publishing conglomerates that churn out hundreds or thousands of books every year in virtually every book category, even down to small or medium-sized indie publishing houses—which are popular for curating more focused lists of book releases or specialize only in very specific genres and categories.

Self-publishing

When you have the liberty to decide whatever services or suppliers you want to contract to have your book printed, then you're on the path to self-publishing. Self-publishing has allowed many authors to have their book printed and reach their target audience regardless of how big or small their platform is. It has levelled the playing field for every aspiring author who wants to publish their book, albeit for a price.

Unlike traditional publishing, you are responsible for financing, marketing, and the entire decision-making process while publishing your book. Nonetheless, many self-published authors have had significant success that has enabled them to secure lucrative traditional publishing deals.

The cost of self-publishing a book varies based on the platform and the format, but what remains consistent is the freedom to publish your book without any restrictions. Due to this, authors who self-publish their work can retain full creative control. Aside from the freedom it gives, another advantage of self-publishing is that it allows authors to receive all future profits from books sales.

Hybrid publishing

Hybrid publishing typically combines the traditional publishing and self-publishing approach. By choosing this path, both the authors and publishers share the risks of launching the book to the market. Similar to traditional publishers, there is a level of expectations required from the author by the publisher as they can dictate the editorial criteria.

Hybrid publishers often request little or no advance payments from authors and offer higher royalty rates when compared to traditional publishers. There's also the option of choosing from different promotional packages that the author can purchase.

Many aspiring authors may choose traditional publishers for the sole reason that they can benefit from a certain level of brand trust or equity in the marketplace and with readers. However, authors must also be willing to give up control of their book and accept lower royalties on book sales. On the flip side, with self-publishing and hybrid publishing, you have more creative control of your work and higher royalties, even though you have to bear some or all the responsibility for how your book performs in the market. If you are not familiar with the publishing industry or don't have that much marketing and social media experience, choosing the latter options can pose a challenge.

How to choose

Before choosing your desired publishing path, it is necessary to ask yourself some critical questions. Is your book written in a way that appeals to a broad audience? How much are you willing to invest in getting your work published? Do you have the required skills and patience to successfully launch a high-quality book? Thinking about these questions would help in determining your target audience and ultimately, your publishing path.

Most successful writers would agree with Jerry Jenkins,[6] a 21-time New York Times bestselling author, when he advises, "Please exhaust all efforts to be traditionally published before resorting to self-publishing. If you are fortunate enough to have your manuscript accepted by a traditional publishing house, they assume all the financial risk, so it costs you nothing."

Should you still choose the path of self-publishing or hybrid publishing, the cost of doing so varies greatly. Ultimately, your readers are the most important piece in the puzzle, so it is necessary to ensure that your book is properly written and edited before launch.

CHAPTER 2

YOUR AUTHOR BUSINESS PLAN

If you've chosen the path of self-publishing, then your job is no longer just writing. As an aspiring author, you have to transform your passion for writing into a business and you will need to have an effective strategy in place.

In the world of self-publishing, you have to become your own CEO. Without a business plan to clarify your goals and guide your actions, it would be impossible to succeed. Having a business plan as an author can help you easily clarify and document a clear vision for your career which in turn would guide all of your business decisions. It would also help you filter out distractions and determine all that you'll need to achieve your desired goal.

By dedicating quality time to create and review your business plan, you can instantly change the trajectory of your writing career for the best. So, before you launch into the self-publishing path, it is important to have a clearly written business plan that will help guide your actions and clarify your goals at every defined interval.

Mission statement

You need to clearly state what your values and vision for your writing business would be. To create a valid mission statement, you must determine the reason why you write and the desired impact of your work.

A mission statement isn't just a goal: it is a strong statement that steers you towards your ultimate goal. Let readers know what your promise to them is and how you intend to deliver on it through your mission statement. You can also include a vision statement as an inspiration and a constant reminder of your commitment.

Author brand and culture

As a writer, it is important to define what your brand is as it enables you to determine how readers relate to your work. Today, brands like Nike are known for a particular range of products and experiences, and this is something that you can build with your work.

To achieve this, you need to build a brand that expresses a particular feeling when people come in contact with either your book, a blog post from you, or yourself when you speak at a public event. Elements such as your writing tone, choice of colours, values, and visuals can reflect the type of branding you want.

Once you have created a brand for yourself, your community of readers can have a certain expectation from you in terms of your voice, writing style, professionalism, and authenticity. It is critical to build a brand that is relevant to your target audience.

Ideal reader

The whole purpose of publishing a book is to get it in the hands of readers. Therefore, your plan has to clearly define this group of people whom you want to reach.

Having a good knowledge of your target audience is important to the growth of your writing career. It becomes much easier to create relevant, valuable, and interesting content when you know exactly what your audience is searching for. Besides, it's almost impossible to create a marketing and promotion plan without having a clue of who might be most interested in your message.

Ultimately, your goal is to try to understand and define what your readers want and align your plan accordingly. Remember, you should focus on *their* main problems and not yours—and don't attempt to force an interest where there's none.

Career goals and objectives

There are very few people who write down their goals, but it's been shown that people who do are more likely to accomplish them.

In a 10-year study carried out during a Harvard MBA program,[7] students who wrote down their goals achieved significantly more than those who didn't—earning on average 10 times more than the other 97 per cent of the class combined. So, writing down your career goals and objectives is a huge step in accomplishing them.

Ensure that your goals are S.M.A.R.T.[8] (Specific, Measurable, Achievable, Relevant and Time-based,) and that you can put in the required effort to achieve all that you've set out to achieve.

Market analysis

Take time to research who are the best-selling authors and influencers in your chosen genre or niche. It's important to draw up a list of people who have already attracted the audience you want to reach. By studying these people, you can learn a thing or two about how to effectively market your brand.

For example, if your competitors are using social media marketing strategies, you can leverage this and craft your personal execution strategy. You need to ask yourself what they are doing right and how you can improve upon it.

Taking note of current trends and predictions in the industry may also have an impact on your overall success. It can help you determine where there may be chances for collaboration or partnership, whether within your chosen genre or with other businesses that service your target audience.

Differentiator

After learning all you need to know about your target market and target audience, it is necessary to create a merger between your unique offering and your reader's expectations or needs.

Knowing what your readers can get from your book that isn't available anywhere else would make you stand out. The ultimate goal is to provide the perfect answer to the question lingering in every reader's mind: "Why you and not them?"

Once you can develop a compelling brand story that solves a unique problem and adequately portrays the uniqueness of your work, you'll have an advantage.

Financials

It can be very easy lose control of the financials for those who are new to the self-publishing path and lack proper guidance. Therefore, it is important to define what your budget would be for all the activities you intend to carry out.

Given the goals you set for your writing business, it is important to benchmark the cost of your work by employing a suitable pricing strategy. Your overall business plan should not only include how much you're willing to spend to publish and promote your book, but also the pricing structure for selling it.

Action steps

Carefully break down your self-publishing path into solid actionable steps[9] in the order in which you intend to carry them out.

From editing, to finding a self-publishing partner, to defining financials, to running marketing campaigns, and to much more, once you itemize your action plan, it gives you a vivid picture of what the next phase in your execution should be.

The final section of your author business plan should be an indicator of what you intend to do next after launching. That way, you can decide if you intend to focus on post-launch engagements or start working on your next manuscript.

CHAPTER 3

YOUR BOOK'S CONCEPTION

Getting into the right headspace

So, you have an idea and have decided to write a book about it. In today's world, authors have the power to change thousands, and even millions of lives through their work.

Figuring out how to write a book from the beginning till the end can be quite daunting, especially when all you have is just a lingering idea and a blank page. Even the best authors would tell you that it is much easier to quit than to actually finish writing a book.

Many writers fail to finish writing a book because they eventually run out of ideas, start getting bored about their message, become distracted, procrastinate or get overwhelmed by the scope of the task before them. However, this can all be a mindset problem. Bestselling author and entrepreneur Tony Robbins has explained that achieving success in anything is 80 per cent psychological and 20 per cent strategic: "what we really have to do is get ourselves to follow through, and the reason why most people don't follow through is because their psychology is messed up."[10]

Writing a book can feel like a huge project. But, rather than focusing on your book being a 600-page monstrosity, look at it as a series of chapters with series of paragraphs. Always see your book for what it truly is: a manuscript made up of different phrases, sentences, paragraphs, pages, and chapters. Once you can eliminate the thought that you're writing one colossal project, it becomes easier start to realize how everything begins to add up very quickly, page by page. Even that 600-page monster can be completed in a few mere months.

It is important to keep your thought process simple. Begin by breaking down your big idea from one page to a single sentence that acts as your premise. However, before you can do this, you need to properly settle on what exactly your big idea for your book is.

Finding your great inspiration

Writing requires passion, and your book idea needs to be something you're passionate about. It should not only be exciting to you, but to every other person you share it with. If you are struggling to finish your book after multiple attempts, it's possible that your idea isn't right for a book, but you may be able to rework it for a different presentation— a short story, a blog post, an essay, or perhaps a video.

But how do you know you have an idea worth writing a book about? Well, you need to ask yourself if it's captivating enough to keep growing in your mind each time you think of it. Don't be shy of sharing your ideas with family, friends, and mentors who can give you an honest opinion and valuable advice.

If you need proof of how much a little, exciting idea can grow over time, just look at the huge success of the *Harry Potter* series of books. J.K. Rowling has talked at length about the development of those stories and how she was inspired to turn a childhood fantasy into one of the media giants of our age: "One weekend after flat hunting, I took the train back to London on my own and the idea for Harry Potter fell into my head," said J.K. Rowling when speaking to *Urbanatte*[11] on how the idea for Harry Potter began. "I had been writing since I was six, but I had never been as excited about an idea as I was for this book."

Make a plan and a schedule

Once you're certain that your idea is promising enough to be written, the next thing to do is to have a plan. For writers, that entails drafting a book outline. This provides a clear vision of the direction in which your book should go.

Not every writer is keen on developing outlines. Many writers of fiction describe themselves as pantsers, as in flying by the seat of their pants as they write. These are authors who write their first draft in a way that doesn't exactly portray the final direction of their work. Despite the success some find with this supposedly freewheeling approach, there is still some underlying sense of direction. Every author needs a basic structure to their work, and there are different kinds of outlines you can employ to help you.

You can either create very detailed outlines with relevant sentences for every action that would occur in each scene, or you can choose to make basic bullet points of your main ideas. For pantsers, a bullet point outline is the best approach since they can provide a lot of flexibility as the work progresses.

In addition to an outline, it is vital that you carry out adequate research, no matter whether you're writing a fiction or non-fiction. Research ensures that the details, whether logical, technical, imaginative, or historical, are accurate and believable.

Once you have created your book outline, bearing in mind that it is still a flexible document, the next thing you need to do is create a writing schedule. Renowned bestselling author Jerry Jenkins recommends that you dedicate at least six hours every week to your book, breaking it down into different sessions that work for you. "I recommend a regular pattern (same times, same days) that can most easily become a habit. But if that's impossible, just make sure you carve out at least six hours so you can see real progress," said Jenkins.[12]

It is necessary to hold yourself accountable and be committed to finishing your book by setting a deadline. Therefore, your writing schedule should align with the deadline you have chosen, and this would help you stay disciplined during the writing process.

A lot of writers find it difficult to keep to their writing schedule due to the presence of numerous distractions. After writing one or two sentences, you find yourself surfing through your email, replying to a comment on social media, or having a lengthy conversation with a friend.

These are all insidious timewasters that would eventually slow down your writing process and even lead to writer's block. Find areas in and around your house where you can minimize distractions and focus on your writing project.

CHAPTER 4

YOUR ROAD TO FINANCIAL SUCCESS

Pre-marketing build-up

If you're wondering what premarketing is, you are not alone. Many writers prefer not to think of the business side of their work, but it is a necessary consideration. If you want people to read your work, then you must let them know it exists. What better way than to have a pre-engaged audience, waiting with enthusiasm for the release of a book whose ending you probably haven't even figured out yet.

Premarketing[13] is the foundational stage of any marketing plan before a product or service is marketed, launched, or published. In the context of marketing a book, premarketing is the set of actions a writer takes to engage an audience before finishing or selling a book. The writer creates awareness of who they are with a target audience and like-minded thinkers. This is not a profit-oriented exercise because it is mainly intended to create a connection with your audience and your message.

There is a saying that goes, "your craft is valid, find a market that agrees." Pre-marketing is a way to find that market, which has not only grown to trust you, but is also psyched to take on whatever you bring you to the table.

Building a premarketing plan and your target audience

Understand who you're writing for and why. Who are the people it will inspire, the audience it will educate, the colleagues with a shared interest, the demographic most suitable for the material? Having a clear picture of your audience can easily help you create something that will resonate with them while building anticipation for what you have to offer.

While social media can seem overwhelming and time-draining, there are simple ways to engage and build your audience through actions and conversations that cut the boundaries of your writing. The next steps highlight these:

Set your objective

If you can think of what goal you want to achieve with your writing, besides making a name and some good money, then you're on your way to building the right engagement strategy. A clear vision of your writing style and values can help you create the best marketing information and foster the right partnerships and associations for your work.

Create your website

The truth is that a basic website will do just fine. Have a simple platform where your audience can learn about you and your works, see updates on upcoming projects, subscribe to your newsletters, connect to your social media handles, and generally have a feel of what you're about as a writer. You may also want to create a blog to upload new content and keep yourself in people's minds.

Make your message bold and visible on the first page of your website and have quick navigations to direct your visitors on your platform.

Build an email list

A sure way to retain and build a connection with people who have already shown interest in you and your work is by sending regular newsletters and updates to their emails. This avails them the opportunity to stay conversant with you and work, so you require no further introduction when the book is published. You can build your email lists by asking visitors to subscribe to your newsletters or other updates on your website and social media posts.

Send out newsletters

If you're a giver who is ready to dish out relevant information to your audience, mostly for free, you'll be surprised how much your newsletters will be anticipated by your growing audience.

Set the frequency at which you want to send out newsletters and updates and stick to them. Your newsletters must be appealing, filled with relevant content, interesting, friendly, and casual. It should also contain a catchy subject line, social/contact Information, and a call to action.

A newsletter is a good content marketing tool, so be sure to keep yours polished and of good quality. Preview your work, describe your process, provide tips, and share ideas, relevant links, and questionnaires. This kind of newsletter is essential to marketing yourself and your art. Your newsletter creates a bridge to your audience, so it should also be educative and helpful to your subscribers.

Let your guard down

While an expository on your personal life is not required, your truth as a writer is. Your audience should be able to meet the same person on paper and in person. Nothing would build a stronger trust and connection with your audience than letting them in to discover you as an individual and as a writer. Your vulnerabilities, struggles with the piece, delays, rough drafts, timelines, excerpts, and work processes all lead them on a journey and help you build a committed reading family, ready to buy into your first publication.

Keep at it!

Patience and consistency are sure ways to attain success and grow at anything, including marketing. You never know who will reach out because of a piece you wrote several years ago, so stay accessible through your works and platforms.

While you may have a niche audience, it can grow over time if you stay visible, true to your vision, and consistent in quality. So keep writing while growing your platforms and reach.

CHAPTER 5

WRITING IT: EXECUTING YOUR BOOK

Write a book within 24 hours or more?

The most difficult part of becoming an author isn't getting your work published, but in the actual writing. Books don't write themselves and for many aspiring authors, getting their book written in time is quite a challenge.

Every year, there are millions of books left unfinished. These are books that could have gone a long way in helping people and leaving a positive impact on the world. But, for one reason or another, the author quit. The journey to writing a book is an amazingly creative process, but most people who want to write a book end up not doing so—either due to procrastination or taking the wrong approach while writing.

In other words, as an aspiring author, your writing process matters a lot. You must not only finish your book, but write one that's good enough to be sold. And if you want to increase your chances of finishing your book, you need to have a proven plan. Like bestselling author Jeff Goins said, "Before you can launch a bestseller, first you have to write one."[14]

The ideology that a bestseller has to be 500-pages long is wrong and can be discouraging for most writers. You don't need to write a very wordy book before you can provide value to your reader. In fact, there are a lot of voluminous books in the market today but with as high as 90 per cent of the content being below par—and no reader wants to waste their time reading such books. Instead of aiming for long projects, start small and write short collections of stories or poems.

First, decide what you want your book to be about and write down the argument in one sentence. Then you can slowly stretch it out into paragraphs, and then to a one-page outline, after which you can create a table of content. Doing this will act as a guide when you write, and it allows you to divide your book into sentences, paragraphs, chapters, and sections. Whenever you want to write a book, think of it in terms of having a beginning, middle, and end. Anything else would make it more complicated.

When you break down a book into more structured bits, it becomes a lot easier to finish it in a shorter period of time. All you have to do is immerse yourself into the idea that you have created, and it becomes a lot easier to complete the book in 24 hours or less.[15]

It also helps to set a daily word count goal for yourself. A page a day is approximately 300 words, and this implies you don't actually need to write a lot, you just need to write consistently. Consistency promotes creativity, and by setting a daily target, you'll have something to benchmark your performance against. Ensure it is something attainable so as to help you keep building momentum until your book is finished.

Preventing writer's block

Once you start writing, you'll inevitably face moments of self-doubt, start feeling overwhelmed, or face a host of other obstacles. Being proactive by anticipating these obstacles ensures you will be ready when they eventually come.

One common mistake writer's make that leads to writer's block is seeking perfection, which is quite damaging, especially during a first draft.

"I experience writer's block when I'm trying to write the first draft and I feel that what I write is not going to be good. I'm afraid to be disappointed and embarrassed," says Aya Matsuda,[16] an associate professor at Arizona State University.

While writing, don't try to be the creator and editor at the same time. Leave whatever changes that need to be made until you're done writing. On your first draft, just focus solely on turning the ideas in your head into words, no matter how grammatically incorrect or disorganized they may appear.

For every writer, nothing feels worse than when you're done writing a book and then having to rewrite it because it didn't meet anyone's expectations. To avoid falling victim to this, you should have a few trusted advisers take a look at your work at certain intervals to determine if it is actually worth writing. These can either be your friends, family, or editors. Just ensure you find someone who will give you honest feedback very early in your writing journey to confirm that you're moving in the right direction.

The truth is, no one cares about the book you almost wrote or nearly finished. Everyone only cares about reading a book that was actually finished; and to qualify as a writer, you not only need to be able to start your project but complete it.

You may be tempted to ask, "how do I know if my book is ready?" Well, the short answer is, you really don't. But if you've done all you need to do and put in the required amount of work in completing your book, then just take that final leap of faith by believing in what you've created.

CHAPTER 6

READY-SET-GO: OVERVIEW OF GETTING YOUR BOOK PRODUCED

So, you've finished writing your book and now looking to get it published. Unlike traditional publishing, self-publishing makes it very easy for writers to get their work in front of their readers without spending lots of time going through a rigorous approval process.

Today, the internet has made it possible for anyone to write a book and distribute it to hundreds of millions of readers at little or no cost. The challenge is making these books become bestsellers without the influence and marketing might of a traditional publishing house like HarperCollins behind them. Some writers have risen to the challenge, but many other self-published authors—especially those who are in a haste to get their book produced—can easily overlook the key principles of success, leading to the failure of their books in achieving the desired sell-out rate.

Even with self-publishing, it is very important to choose the right platform as many aspiring authors make the wrong choice. Despite the widespread adoption of self-publishing amongst writers, only a few self-published books actually achieve their sales target.

Almost every independent author has to choose between two routes when getting their book produced: DIY or Assisted. In the DIY approach, the author is responsible for doing everything themselves, including proofreading and editing their manuscript, designing the book cover, formatting, and marketing their books to different platforms.

There are very few, if any, writers out there who can carry out all these activities themselves without the help of professionals. The publishing process is quite delicate and usually overseen by several professionals with years of experience in their field. Therefore, producing a successful book by oneself is almost impossible to achieve.

The next and most suitable option is the assisted approach. With this, writers who want to self-publish can choose from a wide range of professional editors, proofreaders, designers, and book marketers to work with. Because prudent independent authors are confined to work with a limited budget, they will try to learn and do as much as they can by themselves. Once you've improved your manuscript as far as you can on your own, it becomes necessary to bring in a fresh pair of eyes by hiring the services of a professional to handle everything outside your expertise.

Assistance for your self-publishing goals

Now, with professional guidance, self-publishing platforms like AgoraPublishing.com stand out from the rest particularly because of their commitment to ensuring that your work is of top quality, allowing it to attain mass marketability effortlessly.

Based out of Ottawa, Canada, Agora Publishing is a not-for-profit book publishing agency that supports self-publishing authors to achieve their book sales target. The agency has been in operation for over 20 years, consistently serving writers all around the globe who seek to take advantage of their numerous full-service options which are not provided by other competing platforms like Lulu or CreateSpace.

Agora Publishing has built a successful roadmap for its authors, which includes their book production and marketing strategies. Their team of professionals works with independent authors to produce high-quality books and attract the attention of readers. The agency provides a host of professional community-driven services and their book production process can be highlighted in series of steps.

The first step in getting your book produced is having your manuscript evaluated. Doing this helps iron out any issues with your manuscript by making structural edits to refine the plot, characterization, and voice for fiction, or content, argument, and organization for non-fiction. At the same time, a professional copy editor will also take note of errors in spelling, grammar, punctuation, and style—even down to phrases or passages that appear awkward or anachronistic.

After proper editing, you would then need to complete your book's ISBN registration before typesetting. According to Agora Publishing, "one rookie mistake that many self-published writers make is that they don't have the beginning of their chapter lined up correctly, even after passing it through multi-billion-dollar self-publishing corporations."[17]

Even with a high-quality manuscript, having a bad book cover can contribute to poor sales. Some independent authors try to cut cost by patronizing cheap homemade book cover designers. An amateurish cover is sure to turn off readers and affect sales. Most readers still judge a book by its cover—especially cheap-looking books. Therefore, it is important to get the best quality book cover design to portray the book's worth.

Engaging in premarketing activities is what generates the right amount of buzz for your upcoming book. Luckily, there are many tried-and-true methods that you can use in promoting your title. These include writing and publishing Google-trending and newspaper-style promotional articles, designing a book website and author's news blog, and by performing search engine optimization (SEO) and search engine marketing (SEM).

You can also get other authors' reviews on your book and conduct pre-launch interviews to boost marketing efforts. After deciding which format to produce your book in—whether paperback or e-book—you can distribute it through various online and traditional channels.

Racing into the world of self-publishing can hit you with a cruel reality when your book runs up against the thousands of competing titles. The best chance for success is having a proper pre-and-post production plan to help your book stand out. Thankfully, platforms like AgoraPublishing.com provides writers with free professional consultation and expert services, handling the entire production process for you. This way, your book goes through rigorous quality checks to ensure that only the best version is made available to the public.

CHAPTER 7

NITTY GRITTY FACETS OF PRE-MARKETING

As an aspiring author, it can be difficult to determine just when to market your new book. However, one rule of thumb is to start promotion as early as you can. This helps generate genuine interest in your work before it's even launched—similar to how movies are promoted before they hit the big screens.

By putting in the right amount of effort to reach your audience and building up loyalty before your launch date, you're going to be able to hit the ground running once you are finally ready to sell. There are several pre-launch marketing strategies that you can employ to help you achieve this.

Book cover design

Your book cover can be a powerful marketing tool that can significantly influence your sales and knowing how to use it to your advantage is crucial.

Leaving a great first impression makes a huge difference, whether it's a first date, a job interview, or your book release. One way to catch readers attention in an industry saturated with endless variety of books is by creating an attractive and professional book cover. To achieve this, always ensure that your book cover provides enough clarity as to what the book is about and what genre it falls into.

To do this effectively, you have to carefully articulate the vision of the book to the designer in a way that they can understand it just as clearly as the intended audience. The main goal of your book cover should be providing clarity on what the book is about, and you can check similar self-published titles in your genre for inspiration.

According to research carried out by Reedsy,[18] books that have professionally crafted covers get an approximately 35 per cent increase in marketability. Your book cover design can be much more than just a beautiful work of art. It can be used in numerous ways to support your pre-marketing campaign, such as by hosting a book cover reveal on social media, creating a book trailer, including it in your newsletter and pre-order links, and printing it on author merchandise.

Author blogs/book websites

One of the most powerful marketing tools you can possess when launching your book is an author website. Internet usage is growing[19] and anyone who doesn't own a website when marketing their product or service loses credibility to direct competition that does. But why exactly does an author need a website?

An author's website is the hub of all their activities and the foundation of every pre-and-post marketing book project. Having a website allows writers to have a centralized space to house all their content online, share details about upcoming events, engage with fans, and essentially build their brand image. Many writers assume that the most important part of being an author is being able to write a great book. In reality, building the right audience is almost as important.

By creating a website and publishing short articles on your blog consistently, writers can actively build a strong following before or during their writing process. That way, they already have a group of people patiently anticipating their book's release date.

Writers can keep their audience engaged by sharing behind-the-scenes moments, book inspiration, a catalogue of books they're currently reading, contributing on topics within their expertise, and sharing details of the places they love to explore.

Search engine optimization for authors

If you have already created your author website or blog, the next thing that you should be working on is search engine optimization (SEO). Simply put, SEO is an organic and free way for websites to receive more traffic. This entails figuring out what kinds of search terms people might use if they were the right audience for your book and making sure that they find you when they use a search engine. Effectively, if the keywords are there in a reasonable amount on your website, then you'll appear high in relevant keyword searches.

If someone goes to Google and types in "top sci-fi books in 2021," ideally you would want your website to show up on the first page. Generally, ranking on page 1 of Google is the best because almost 90 per cent of users[20] don't click beyond that—realistically, you might get to page 2 of Google, but most people never get to page 3.

Authors who use the right SEO strategy can drive quality traffic to their website and invariably increase their email newsletter signups and book sales. SEO can definitely feel overwhelming at first, but there are simple tips you can use to build the right strategy.

Keyword research allows you develop the right content to attract more visitors. By choosing the right focused keywords, you can quickly take your blog page views from zero to hundreds of thousands. Nonetheless, you can have the best keywords in the world on your website, but they won't be of much use if your content isn't actually helpful. Therefore, you need to make sure the content you're creating is relevant to your audience.

Also, don't be afraid to experiment with different keywords on your website. Take note of which posts drive the most traffic and have the most engagement. That way you can focus on improving on what works and trying something else if it doesn't.

Pre-ordering strategies

One common book marketing strategy is to set up a pre-order offer for your upcoming book or eBook. Including pre-order campaigns into your book marketing plan can definitely help you build enough buzz before your book launch. Plus, they are a great way to engage existing fans and attract new ones. When done right, pre-orders can be highly influential in boosting overall sales.

Pre-ordering can be relatively easy to set up with a self-publishing platform such as Amazon's Kindle Direct Publishing (KDP).[21] Other strategies such as a pre-order giveaway, sharing digital swag, offering discounts, and running contests are also effective.

Ensure that you start planning for your pre-launch early, so you will already have a marketing plan in place when your book is eventually ready for pre-sale.

CHAPTER 8

IMPORTANT PRODUCTION CONSIDERATIONS

Getting your book produced takes a series of important yet delicate steps. Below are some of the most important things to consider during your book publishing process.

ISBN registration

One topic that always comes up during the book publishing process is how to get an ISBN. While it is true that not every author gets thrilled by the idea of acquiring a serial number but, just like proofreading and editing, it is a crucial part of self-publishing.

An International Standard Book Number,[22] or ISBN, is a 13-digit code used as an internationally accredited unique identifier for books. It is fixed code that is non-transferable, which basically means that even if you publish the same book in both a paperback and eBook format, you will need to get separate ISBNs for each format. Additionally, if you decide to publish the eBook in a different language, you'll also need to get a new ID for that version.

An ISBN is typically assigned to each edition of a publication, allowing libraries, readers, publishers, and bookstores to quickly find specific titles. Most online retailers, bookstores, libraries, wholesalers, and distributors use this unique identifier to keep track of book purchases and sales. Without one, your ability to sell your book is extremely limited.

However, if you intend to publish only as an eBook, then an ISBN may or may not be needed. Some of the most popular online retailers such as Amazon, Kobo, Apple, and Barnes & Noble don't mandate authors provide an ISBN when submitting an eBook, especially since they provide their own unique identifier. Therefore, if you plan to sell an eBook through these retail channels, then you can skip getting an ISBN.

Depending on where you live, the cost of acquiring an ISBN can vary since each country has its own agency responsible for issuing ISBNs. In the US, Bowker is the official ISBN agency, while authors in the UK can acquire it from Nielsen. In some countries, including Canada,[23] ISBNs are issued for free.

Basic copy editing

Copy editing ensures important elements in your manuscript such as spelling, grammar, punctuation, and syntax are accurate. It also checks to ensure that your style and tone is consistent throughout the entire document and that your choice of words and language is easily understood by your target audience. In fact, copy editing is so important that skipping it drastically lowers the quality of your book.

Professional copy editors provide the required expertise. Since they are not necessarily subject-matter experts, they can easily notice when certain information is missing in your text or when your concepts are ambiguous. A copy editor has the necessary skills to help authors rewrite an entire passage, and the feedback they provide to authors is invaluable.

Copy editing has a huge impact on a writer's manuscript, but it is both tedious and misguided for an author to copy edit their work themselves. Being too close to the writing makes writers unable to spot major problems, whether related to the mechanics of writing or the content itself. If you must choose between proofreading and copy editing due to budget constraints, copy editing should be your go-to option.

Advanced copy editing considerations

As an aspiring author, you can easily get confused over the different meaning of editing in the publishing industry, especially since they are often used interchangeably. However, when hiring a professional editor, there are advanced copy editing terms[24] to always keep in mind.

Line editing

One term that is often used interchangeably with copy editing is line editing. However, it is quite different from copy editing as it refers to a type of editing that is more intense. When line editing, the editor reviews your manuscript line by line, analyzing each sentence carefully for grammatical, structural, and spelling errors. The editor examines your choice of words and the meaning and impact of a sentence on your text.

A line editor would review your syntax and determine which sentence needs to be rephrased or removed.

Developmental editing

If you're thinking of how to ensure there's consistency with the big picture in your book, then developmental editing handles this. The editor reviews everything from the characters, plots, dialogue, and reader's perspective. Any part of the book that appears weak is scrutinized.

A developmental editor asks crucial questions such whether the characters are relatable, the chapters and paragraphs align correctly, or the pacing lags in the story. The editor considers every aspect of the manuscript making sure the final book is enjoyable and makes sense.

Developmental editing takes a lot of time to complete and is more expensive than other types of editing.

Substantive Editing

This type of editing is focused on the organization and presentation of your text. Substantive editing involves clarifying and restructuring a sentence, paragraph, chapter, and scene. Unlike developmental editing, which is focused on fixing issues with the big picture and deeper restructuring, substantial editing tackles problems with the actual prose of your book.

Substantive editing often gets referred to as line editing and can equally be confused with developmental editing. Therefore, it is important to confirm from your editor what editing types would be used in reviewing your work.

Professional Typesetting

Simply put, typesetting is the process of arranging text, pictures, and graphs onto a page. At this stage of book production—which typically occurs towards the tail end—the typesetter arranges the book's interior in a way that creates the best reading experience. A professional typesetter is responsible for selecting the right fonts, arranging the paragraph, word, line, letter spacing and justification.

Typesetting your book ensures that it meets the required criteria before printing, checking for consistency in your work. For many aspiring authors, the main element of their book is mostly the front cover, but the interior design is just as important and requires the same amount of attention.

Before you send your book out to the printers, you need to be sure that you have proper typesetting done on your manuscript. It would be a huge mistake to underestimate the importance of typesetting as it not only affects your book's readability, but equally impacts its sales.

"Good typesetting isn't obvious — done well it's invisible. Readers should be able to look up from reading to discover they've missed their stop or missed their bedtime, and, most importantly, don't mind," says Annabel Brandon,[25] a specialist in typesetting and typography.

Before finalizing the print-ready files, certain elements of your book need to be checked[26] during typesetting. These include quality control—which covers the basics including appearance, page numbering, and dimensions—page makeup, page design, fonts, tables, illustrations, and index.

What is an eBook?

An eBook is any longer text that has been presented in a digital format, allowing it to be read on a variety of devices such as a computer, mobile phone, or tablet. Many published paperback books have also been made available in eBooks, including bestsellers.

eBooks are used by authors to either bypass print or to make out-of-print titles available to readers. They usually contain only electronic text, but they may also contain some extras, such as video, audio, or hyperlinks.

eBook formatting

There are some common eBook formats and frankly, none of them is better or worse than each other—they are only best suited to different devices. Some of the popular eBook formats are:

PDF: This is ideal for reading on a computer but may be difficult to view on smaller devices like a smartphone. However, it is the cheapest and easiest eBook format to produce.

EPUB: Electronic Publication, commonly referred to as EPUB is the most popular eBook format and can be viewed on any device—the only exception is Amazon's Kindle.

MOBI: This was designed specifically for the Amazon Kindle and works great when accessed with it. Its only limitation is not being accessible on a device that doesn't have the Kindle App installed.

AZW/AZW3: This format belongs to Amazon's publishing platform, so if you're planning to sell your book there, then it should be your most preferred format. This format works well on the Kindle or Kindle App, and also on most computers and smartphones.

Your choice of what eBook format to use depends heavily on where you intend to sell it. Though, it's still best to offer readers a wide range of options to choose from.

eBook formatting versus typesetting for printed copies

eBook formatting differs greatly from printed copies because they are designed to accommodate simple text and layout, as opposed to printed copies that can be designed with beautiful script fonts, styled quotes outside defined text margins, and other unique features.

You are bound to encounter issues trying to format your eBook to appear the same as a printed copy due to issues such as fancy fonts and scripts defaulting to a serif font, inability to place anything outside the text margins, and columns and tabs not working properly.

It is important to work with a designer who has experience creating both digital and print files if you want to get rid of some of these issues.

What about audiobooks?

Audiobooks are voice recordings of the text within a book that allows users to listen rather than read the book. Audiobooks can either be the exact version of the books or a more abridged version. These can be accessed from a computer, tablet, smartphone, or speaker.

For many readers out there, making time to read the books they love can be difficult. Now, with the growing number of audiobooks available, it has quickly become a more convenient alternative to traditional reading.

People can listen to their favourite bestseller while cleaning, commuting, or relaxing. But how similar is listening to a book than reading it? According to Beth Rogowsky, an associate professor of education at the Bloomsburg University of Pennsylvania, listening to audiobooks feels like cheating.

In a 2016 study,[27] Rogowsky carried out a test to confirm her assumptions. Her research concluded that there were "no significant differences in comprehension between reading, listening, or reading and listening simultaneously."[28]

One of the major things to consider when producing an audiobook is your target market. You need to be sure that there is good enough reception for audiobook by the market you intend to sell to. The global audiobook market is estimated at over $3 billion,[29] with almost 90 per cent of that belonging to the U.S. market alone.

Other things to put into consideration during production are industry trends, voice-over, average audio length, creation and distribution channels, and audience demographics.

CHAPTER 9

FORMATS OF BOOKS

Deciding what format to make your book available in is a decision that every modern-day author has to make. As technology improves, there are now more ways to consume information than ever before; the advantage it provides is being able to determine the best method for you.

The publishing industry has witnessed steady growth in sales of books in all formats with over $26 billion in revenue recorded in 2019 in the U.S. alone—with paperback making up $22.6 billion and eBooks raking in $2.04 billion—according to statistics from the Association of American Publishers.[30]

Another booming market is audiobooks. More and more readers are now choosing to listen to their favourite books on the go, whether during a commute or while carrying out chores. Just like audiobooks, eBooks are also increasingly popular due to how easily accessible they are. But not everyone is a fan of both formats. In fact, reports show that most readers still prefer to read a book the traditional way via paperbacks.

"I think the e-book bubble has burst somewhat, sales are flattening off, I think the physical object is very appealing. Publishers are producing incredibly gorgeous books, so the cover designs are often gorgeous, they're beautiful objects," reports Meryl Halls,[31] managing director of the Booksellers' Association in the U.K.

Before you decide what format to release your book in, here are some of the pros and cons of each one for your readers.

Pros of paperbacks (or hardcovers)

Physical books are not going anywhere anytime soon as readers still prefer it over other book formats. With a paperback, you are not dependent on electricity and can read it for as long as you want. You get that classic new book feeling that isn't quite the same with owning an eBook or audiobook.

For some people, the thrill of owning a book library is incomparable. With paperbacks, you can build a book library that looks very classy. You can also easily lend a physical book to your friends and equally borrow one. There are lots of distractions when reading books on digital devices that you don't get with paperbacks.

Cons of paperbacks (or hardcovers)

One major disadvantage of paperbacks is being unable to read them in the dark. Without proper lighting, reading a physical book can be very challenging. Also, if you live in an apartment with limited space, stacking up physical books would threaten the space in your home. Lastly, when compared to other book formats, paperbacks (and hardcovers) are the most expensive.

Pros of eBooks

The advantages of owning an eBook are quite vast. From the ease of access to decluttering and being easily transferred, eBooks also allow users to access other online book services that connect them to other readers.

eBooks are quite cheap to produce and distribute for authors. And, for those who don't like the idea of a physical library, you can easily build one online.

Cons of eBooks

The major disadvantage of owning an eBook is the distractions that come with it. Depending on what you're reading it with, notification popups can be extremely distracting and can easily steal your focus away from the reading experience.

Another disadvantage of an eBook over paperbacks is that it requires your reader to have a powered device. Without electricity, or internet access, readers can't access your book.

Pros of audiobooks

No matter where you are or what you're doing, as long as you have an internet-enabled device with you, you can easily access your audiobook. It even allows you to multitask effectively, especially with tasks that require little thought, such as cleaning, cooking, or taking a walk.

"People enjoy hearing a voice telling stories to them," suggests Marshall Davis,[32] owner of a sound engineering company, Davis Sound. "With audiobooks, people are allowed to multitask while listening to a story. They look for the emotion and character voice that comes with an audiobook narrator."

Cons of audiobooks

One major turnoff with audiobooks is the relatively large amount of data they require. If you keep stacking up audiobooks, you may need to invest in additional storage for your device.

Also, just like eBooks, audiobooks require a device with a power source. Therefore, if your battery is dying, you won't be able to listen. It is also the most expensive option to create and distribute due to labour costs, voice-actor costs, studio costs, and royalties.

In conclusion, before producing your book, carefully examine the pros and cons of each format and decide which one would be best for you considering your target audience.

CHAPTER 10

PRINT-ON DEMAND VERSUS PRINTING FOR AN INVENTORY

One final step in the book publishing process for authors is determining whether to print your book on-demand or for an inventory. Every self-publishing author needs to be knowledgeable about these two methods since it is crucial to the sales and distribution of their work.

Print-on-demand is when a buyer must place an order for a book so that it can be printed and shipped to them. With this method, there's very limited upfront cost since the author won't have to pay for printing large quantities of a book before putting it on sale. Though the manufacturing cost is significantly higher, authors don't have to worry about renting storage space to house numerous copies of their book. Print-on-demand also allows authors to make any necessary changes to the content of their book even after publishing and selling a few copies.

Choosing the inventory method implies that many copies of your book would be printed and stored, and then shipped to buyers on request. Unlike print-on-demand, this method means authors pay less per copy since the large volume printing reduces the cost per book.

Print-on-demand overview

Based on recent figures,[33] about half of all published book titles sell less than 250 copies annually—with 30 per cent of books produced globally going unsold. That said, print-on-demand (POD) has revolutionized the way the publishing industry carries out its business.

Now, the costs associated with maintaining an inventory of books for independent authors is all but eliminated. Print-on-demand is one of the most efficient and affordable ways to distribute your book, eliminating the need to invest in an initial number of prints.

If you have ever searched for a book in a physical or online bookstore only to discover it's out of print or sold out, then the author most likely used an inventory service. With print-on-demand publishing, copies of books are printed as they are needed. That way, you never run out of stock. It doesn't matter if one person in Canada wants just a copy of your book, or someone else in Germany wants 2000 copies, with print-on-demand, book order management is fast and reliable.

A self-published author who maintains an inventory is forced to do a lot of extra work. When an order is placed for a book, authors would have to pick it from their home storage unit, purchase envelopes or delivery boxes, apply shipping labels, and take it to a delivery service for it to get delivered to the end user's location. This method can be quite expensive especially considering the cost of shipping and supplies. However, with print-on-demand, your book gets printed on order and shipped directly from the print facility to the end-user.

For self-publishers, printers, and even the environment[34], print-on-demand is much better as it eliminates waste because books are printed only when an order is placed.

Getting your self-published book available for sale

Most independent authors choose the flexibility of print-on-demand publishing over the upfront cost of inventory printing. However, there are still some factors to consider, like your printing budget, the type of book you're printing, the quality of the printers, your online distribution plan, and which distributor you intend to use.

To get your self-published book available for sale, you'll need to choose between one or more of the available leading print-on-demand services described below.

IngramSpark

Currently the largest book distributor and wholesaler in the United States,[35] Ingram Book Group has a publishing platform for independent publishers offering services that include production, distribution, and assembling of books.

IngramSpark lets authors publish both digital and physical print-on-demand books, but you must pay a startup fee to get started. Once you have your book uploaded on their platform, it instantly becomes available to over 40,000 libraries and bookstores all over the world.

One major disadvantage of this platform is the steep learning curve for users who must be able to navigate the user interface. Also, unlike other print-on-demand services, IngramSpark won't automatically correct formatting errors. Instead, it only flags errors in formatting, leaving it up to you to make the corrections yourself.

Amazon Kindle Direct Publishing (KDP)

This is the option most publishers look out for when choosing print-on-demand. While it has its downsides, it is also one of the easiest platforms to use. The entire process from signing up to uploading your manuscript and entering your book details takes nothing more than a few minutes.

One downside of this platform is being unable to publish hardcover books since it only supports paperbacks. Nonetheless, in addition to selling paperback versions of your book, you can also sell an eBook version on Amazon Kindle.

You can earn as high as 60 per cent royalty[36] on book sales on Amazon marketplaces in the U.S., Japan, and Europe.

BookBaby

This is a self-publishing platform that provides lots of support to independent authors. Support includes marketing, design, editing, and distribution services. For its print-on-demand service, BookBaby handles payments and shipments for you, and you'll receive your royalties just a few days after your book has been sold.

Unfortunately, BookBaby is an expensive distribution channel and is most ideal for authors who want to supplement their inventory.

Blurb

If you're looking for a print-on-demand company that not only publishes books, but allows you to create and sell other items such as notebooks, magazines, wall art, and trade books, then Blurb is the platform for you.

The Blurb distribution network consists of over 38,000 stores, libraries, and schools, and you can sell your books both on Amazon or Blurb's online bookstore. Blurb is great for printing and distributing visual, image-based books.[37]

It is necessary to plan your book sales and distribution strategy for independent online and offline bookstores ahead of time. Once you know what type of books they sell and to whom, it becomes easy to determine whether or not your book is a good fit for your chosen store.

ADDENDUM

Here are critical general tips for authors who seek to expedite their book self-publishing successfully:

Step 1 - Make sure you get an ISBN. Don't rely on Amazon if you seek international distribution.

Step 2 - Start your marketing campaign before you complete the writing of your manuscript

Step 3 - Get a sample review of a few pages of your manuscript before paying a copy editor

Step 4 - Make sure you choose an amazing book cover design that is essential to marketing

Step 5 - Never skip out on excellent typesetting if you want a professional look

Step 6 - Use a mixture of social media to promote your book

Step 7 - Create an author blog as the centre of your social media marketing strategy

Step 8 - A well-updated blog can generate supplementary revenue

Step 9 – To increase sales, try to devote some time on a daily basis to promotion

Step 10 - Use YouTube as part of your social media marketing strategy

ENDNOTES

1   Lydia T. Blanco, "Meet the Self-Published Author Who Negotiated A Deal with Netflix," Forbes Women, 9 December 2020. https://www.forbes.com/sites/lydiatblanco/2020/12/09/meet-the-self-published-author-who-negotiated-a-deal-with-netflix/?sh=4e7db25e1507

2   Andre Perrin, "Who Doesn't Read Books in America," 26 December 2019. https://www.pewresearch.org/fact-tank/2019/09/26/who-doesnt-read-books-in-america/

3   Lauren Hughes, "How to Overcome Writer's Block: 20 Helpful Tips," Reedsyblog, 6 November 2019. https://blog.reedsy.com/writers-block/

4   Perry Marshall, "How to Use the 80/20 Rule to Work Less and Make More," Everyone Hates Marketers, 7 May 2019. https://www.everyonehatesmarketers.com/podcast/80-20-rule-marketing

5   Ingrid Beck, "Publishing Pros and Cons: Traditional vs Self vs Hybrid," The Bindery, 26 September 2019. https://www.thebinderyagency.com/blog/2019/9/26/publishing-pros-and-cons-traditional-vs-self-vs-hybrid

6   Jerry Jenkins, "How to Publish a Book: My Ultimate Guide From 40+ Years of Experience," Jerry Jenkins Blog. https://jerryjenkins.com/how-to-publish-a-book/

7   Ashley Feinstein, "Why You Should Be Writing Down Your Goals," Forbes Women, 8 April 2014. https://www.forbes.com/sites/ellevate/2014/04/08/why-you-should-be-writing-down-your-goals/?sh=77afe97a33972715e4857a0b7a4236e12f14

8   Indeed Editorial Team, "SMART Goals: Definition and Examples," Indeed, 24 November 2020. https://www.indeed.com/career-advice/career-development/smart-goals

9   Kimberly Grabas, "Your Author Business Plan: A Framework for the Creative Entrepreneur," Your Writer Platform, 2 February 2014. https://yourwriterplatform.com/author-business-plan/

10 Kathryn Dill, "Tony Robbins: To Be Truly Successful, Avoid These 3 Mental Traps," CNBC, 21 March 2017. https://www.cnbc.com/2017/03/21/tony-robbins-to-be-truly-successful-avoid-these-3-mental-traps.html

11 Angela Davis, "JK Rowling on Getting Published: Her Fascinating Path from Rags to Riches," Urbanette. https://www.urbanette.com/jk-rowling/

12 Jerry Jenkins, "How to Write a Book from Start to Finish: A Proven Guide," Jerry Jenkins Blog. https://jerryjenkins.com/how-to-write-a-book/

13 Leigh Shulman, "How to Create a Pre-Marketing Plan for Your Writing Life," Leigh Shulman Blog, 6 December 2019. https://leighshulman.com/book-marketing-strategy/

14 Jeff Goins, "10 Ridiculously Simple Steps for Writing a Book," Goins Writer, https://goinswriter.com/tips-writing-book/

15 Stefan James, "How to Write A Book In 24 Hours or Less," Project Life Mastery, 18 March 2021. https://www.youtube.com/watch?v=F034-hDb6m4

16 Elena Shvidko, "How to Overcome Writer's Block: Ideas from Writing Experts," TESOL International Organization Blog, 1 December 2017. http://blog.tesol.org/how-to-overcome-writers-block-ideas-from-writing-experts/

17 Ottawa Book Expo, "How to Self-Publish Your Book - Part 1 - Book Expo Video Podcast," YouTube, 18 May 2020. https://www.youtube.com/watch?v=eM3Q_IDpk_U&t=1853s

18 Reedsyblog, "Revealed: The Real Marketing Value of a Professional Book Cover," 21 September 2017. https://blog.reedsy.com/marketing-value-professional-book-cover/

19 Datareportal, "Digital Around the World," https://datareportal.com/global-digital-overview

20 Pat Ahern, "27 Mind-Bottling SEO Stats for 2021 (+ Beyond)," Intergrowth, 9 April 2021. https://inter-growth.co/seo-stats/

21 Penny Sanseveri, "How to Promote a Self-Published Book with Amazon Pre-Order," Author Marketing Experts, 17 June 2020. https://www.amarketingexpert.com/2020/06/17/how-to-promote-a-self-published-book-with-amazon-pre-order/

22 Editage by Cactus, "10 FAQs on ISBN Every Self-Publishing Author Must Know," https://www.editage.com/info/book-editing-services/articles/10-faqs-on-isbn-every-self-publishing-author-must-know.html

23 Library and Archives Canada (LAC), "ISBN Canada," 19 July 2019. https://www.bac-lac.gc.ca/eng/services/isbn-canada/Pages/isbn-canada.aspx

24 Simon & Schuster, "The Different Types of Editing," Archway Publishing. https://www.archwaypublishing.com/en/resources/the-different-types-of-editing

25 Annabel Brandon, "What is Typesetting? Your Guide to Interior Book Design," Reedsy Blog, 26 October 2018. https://blog.reedsy.com/what-is-typesetting/

26 John Wiley & Sons Inc, "Print-Ready PDFs Preparation," Wiley Inc. https://authorservices.wiley.com/author-resources/book-authors/prepare-your-manuscript/preparing-print-ready-pdfs.html

27 Beth A. Rogowsky, Barbara M. Calhoun, and Paula Tallal, "Does Modality Matter? The Effects of Reading, Listening, and Dual Modality on Comprehension," SAGE Journals, 1 September 2016. https://journals.sagepub.com/doi/full/10.1177/2158244016669550

28 Markham Heid, "Are Audiobooks as Good For You As Reading? Here's What Experts Say," TIME Inc, 6 September 2018. https://time.com/5388681/audiobooks-reading-books/

29 Duncan Stewart, Mark Casey, Craig Wigginton, "The Ears Have it: The Rise of Audiobooks and Podcasting," Deloitte, 9 December 2019. https://www2.deloitte.com/us/en/insights/industry/technology/technology-media-and-telecom-predictions/2020/rise-of-audiobooks-podcast-industry.html

30 Association of American Publishers, "AAP StatShot Annual Report: Book Publishing Revenues Up Slightly to $25.93 Billion in 2019," 31 July 2020. https://publishers.org/news/aap-statshot-annual-report-book-publishing-revenues-up-slightly-to-25-93-billion-in-2019/

31 Lucy Handley, "Physical Books Still Outsell e-books — and Here's Why," CNBC, 19 September 2019. https://www.cnbc.com/2019/09/19/physical-books-still-outsell-e-books-and-heres-why.html

32 Ivy Lariviere, "Preferred Format: eBook, Audiobook, or Print?" September 2018. https://booksmakeadifference.com/book-format/

33 BJ Gallagher, "The Ten Awful Truths — and the Ten Wonderful Truths — About Book Publishing," Huffington Post, 6 December 2017. https://www.huffpost.com/entry/book-publishing_b_1394159

34 Leslie Barton, "Print on Demand: An Earth-Friendly Printing Strategy," Amware Logistics, 21 May 2020. https://www.amwarelogistics.com/blog/earth-friendly-printing-strategy

35 Reedsy Blog, "What is the Best Service for Print on Demand Books?" 13 February 2019. https://blog.reedsy.com/print-on-demand-books/

36 Benjamin Levin, "10 Best Print on Demand For Books 2021," Mofluid. https://mofluid.com/blog/best-print-on-demand-book-sites/

37 Bertel King, "The 4 Best Online Print-on-Demand Book Services for Self-Publishers," MakeUseOf Blog, 16 July 2018. https://www.makeuseof.com/tag/top-4-online-selfpublishers-book-write/

www.ingramcontent.com/pod-product-compliance
Lightning Source LLC
Chambersburg PA
CBHW062159100526
44589CB00014B/1873